HOW MUCH DEFENSE SPENDING IS ENOUGH?

A Rational Debate
sponsored by the American Enterprise Institute
and held at
the Washington Hilton Hotel,
Washington, D.C.

JOHN CHARLES DALY
Moderator

HOW MUCH DEFENSE SPENDING IS ENOUGH?

Jack Kemp
Les Aspin

RATIONAL DEBATE SERIES

American Enterprise Institute for Public Policy Research
Washington, D.C.

ISBN 0-8447-2092-5
Library of Congress Catalog Card Number 76-45561

FOREWORD

From the levies enacted by the Athenians for maintenance of their fleets, through the medieval homage required for the support of nobles in armor, to taxation in modern nations for standing armies, defense has constituted a significant public cost. Judgments about how much to spend and in which areas have often determined the fate of societies.

The question "How much defense spending is enough?" looms heavily for our nation today, when we find ourselves in a world of unprecedented interdependence and destructive capability. A decision about the level of our defense expenditures demands consideration of diverse factors and complex trade-offs.

The participants in this debate, Representatives Aspin and Kemp, express differing views on American defense needs, and both elucidate basic points that require scrutiny. No ultimate answers are found. Their discussion, however, crystallizes issues about which judgments must be made.

The American Enterprise Institute is pleased to present this Rational Debate, the twenty-eighth in its continuing series, on a subject important to the future of America and the world.

September 1976   William J. Baroody
                      President
                      American Enterprise Institute
                        for Public Policy Research

CONTENTS

FIRST LECTURE

JACK KEMP

Since World War II, too many Americans have viewed our national security almost as a matter of inalienable right rather than as something to be earned and preserved through sacrifice and effort. I believe the facts now show that we can no longer take our national security for granted. It is increasingly in jeopardy, and this jeopardy stems primarily from two basic factors.

One factor is the relentless drive of the Soviet Union to achieve military superiority, both in conventional forces and in strategic nuclear weapons. Accompanying this drive is its development of a civil defense program, or, more accurately, a war survival program—which undermines our deterrent strength by lessening Soviet vulnerability to U.S. retaliation.

The other factor is the belief of a great number of Americans that each side has the ability to destroy the other many times over and that, as a consequence, nuclear war would be so devastating that it is unthinkable to the Soviet Union as well as to us. This American belief in "overkill," which is not shared by the Soviet leadership, draws support from the so-called "balance of terror," and makes many Americans question the level of our defense expenditures.

I want to speak to these two factors. Too many people are unwilling to look at the facts. Every credible source, military and civilian, provides evidence of an unprecedented Soviet buildup in strategic and conventional weapons. But there are always those who are eager to tell us that the evidence is all a hoax designed to con the Congress into raising defense expenditures for the benefit of the defense lobby.

The will to disbelieve the obvious is based partly on the inability of peace-loving Americans to come to grips with Soviet tactics and objectives. It is strengthened by the unwillingness of political leaders to admit that the United States is in danger of yielding military superiority to the Soviet Union in strategic and conventional terms and by the exaggerated rhetoric of detente and SALT I (Strategic Arms Limitation Treaty, signed on May 29, 1972).

In the final analysis, how much defense spending is enough depends on our perception of the threat. The danger of the overkill argument is that it blunts that perception.

Just as the French took refuge behind the Maginot Line in the 1930s, a disturbing number of Americans are taking refuge behind "overkill" today. But the overkill argument misses the following points: It deals with weapons in inventory, not with alert, reliable, survivable, penetrating weapons subject to proper command and control. It deals with today's situation rather than that of the critical period five, ten, or fifteen years from now.

Soviet military doctrine and military writings have never accepted, and indeed explicitly reject, the concepts of overkill and of mutual assured destruction. (The latter concept is the basis of the U.S. defense posture.) In the Soviet Union, one does not find the doctrine that once a country possesses a certain nuclear force level, it has nuclear sufficiency to deter an aggressor regardless of the latter's force level. Instead, the Soviet Union emphasizes survivability, and its leaders even talk of victory in nuclear war. They stress that adequate measures can greatly reduce the destructive potential of nuclear weapons and that war remains in the nuclear age a permissible and valid instrument of policy. Perhaps nothing contrasts more starkly with our interpretation of overkill than the fact that the Soviet Union has developed a cold-launch technique for ICBMs that allows missile silos to be reloaded.

This difference in attitudes means many things which are important—indeed crucial—to our defense posture. It means, for example, that we may have more confidence in our deterrent than Moscow has respect for it. The French had greater faith in the Maginot Line than the Germans did, and this difference in assessment led not only to war but to the defeat of France.

It also means that the Soviet Union may be up to different things than we are. Whereas the United States is busy deterring, the U.S.S.R. may be busy preparing for aggression. That is one possible reading, not only of the massive Soviet military buildup and Soviet actions around the world, but also of the comprehensive Soviet program in which population survival measures are combined with the dispersal of key industries, with the construction of underground and hardened industrial sites and hardened facilities for protecting the political leadership, and with establishment of a nationwide command and control structure. If we add to this the U.S.S.R.'s massive air defense system and the emphasis in its strategic doctrine on blunting the enemy's nuclear capability by means of a preemptive first strike, we have some indication that the Soviet Union does not share our commitment to a defensive posture.

Let us look at the kind of misleading calculation upon which our belief in overkill is based. Take, for example, a recent article in the *Bulletin of the Atomic Scientists* in which it is stated that the present stockpile of American nuclear weapons is sufficient to destroy the world's population twelve times over.[1] How did the article arrive at this calculation? It did so by multiplying the casualties per kiloton in Hiroshima and Nagasaki by the total number of kilotons in our nuclear arsenal and dividing by the number of people living in the world. In other words, if the world's population were gathered up and packed together in the same density as existed in Hiroshima and Nagasaki, if that relatively small area were left unwarned and unprotected, and if all our weapons were dropped there, the result would be overkill.

But, defined in this way, overkill is not unique to nuclear weapons. It can exist with conventional explosives as well— and indeed did, both in World War II and in the Vietnam War. During World War II, 10 billion pounds of TNT were dropped on Germany, Japan, and Italy, which comes out to 50 pounds for every man, woman, and child. During the Vietnam War, 25 billion pounds of TNT were dropped—an average of 730 pounds per person.

The United States just does not have an overkill capacity with respect to the Soviet Union, given its enormous expanse, its hardened missile silos, its extensive civil defense program, and the dispersal and hardening of its industry. This conclusion becomes even more clear if we take into account the facts

---

[1] Ruth Leger Sivard, "Let Them Eat Bullets! a statistical portrait of world militarism," in *Bulletin of the Atomic Scientists,* April 1975, p. 6.

that we do not have a first-strike doctrine or capability and that our defense depends on the number of our nuclear weapons that would survive a Soviet attack and be delivered on target. Because we have chosen a defensive posture, we must be able to retaliate after absorbing an attack that would have greatly diminished our strategic forces. A Soviet attack could be successful if it destroyed a lot of our strategic forces and presented unpromising targets, such as evacuated cities and hardened industrial and military facilities, for our remaining forces. In terms of surviving warheads, we do not have overkill. The real question is, At what point does the Soviet strategic buildup put us in a position of "underkill"?

The belief in overkill and the fact of our *current* advantage in nuclear warheads are leading us increasingly to base our security on SALT I and the negotiations for SALT II. In fact, popular wisdom is that SALT is becoming a fourth leg of our defense posture, a substitute for essential defense capabilities. The U.S. secretary of defense and the joint chiefs of staff all testified before the Subcommittee on Defense of the House Appropriations Committee that the fiscal year 1977 defense budget was based in large part on the assumption that the current strategic arms limitation talks would be successful.[2]

Yet it is SALT I itself that legitimized the Soviet Union's advantages in missile throw weight. Critics of U.S. defense spending have emphasized the security provided by our current lead in numbers of warheads, but they fail to point out the offsetting Soviet advantages and trends, ominous advantages

---

[2] U.S. Congress, House, Subcommittee on Defense of the Appropriations Committee, *Defense Appropriations Hearings for FY 1977,* Part I, 94th Cong., 2d sess., 1976.

and trends according to our last three secretaries of defense, Melvin Laird, James Schlesinger, and Donald Rumsfeld.

Those who emphasize our lead today are neglecting the trends that will produce a Soviet lead tomorrow. For example, to count up current numbers of warheads is to count on the basis of the old generation of Soviet ICBMs, and these are currently being replaced with a new generation of ICBMs, the SS-17, SS-18, and SS-19. These new missiles are being MIRVed, that is, fitted with multiple independently targeted reentry vehicles, a development that will increase the number of Soviet ICBM warheads from 1,600 now to 8,400 by the early 1980s. Furthermore, these missiles have warheads whose average yields are five times as great as ours, and they are much more accurate than the ones they replace.

Now some people will ask, Why should we be concerned about the U.S.S.R.'s having nuclear superiority when superiority is not usable anyway? The problem with this position is that the Soviet leaders believe nuclear superiority is usable. Furthermore, once they have it, they will expect to get something out of it through diplomatic intimidation. They not only believe it is usable, but also they know from experience that it is. Former Secretary of State Dean Rusk said, after Soviet Premier Khrushchev had backed down in the confrontation over Soviet nuclear missiles in Cuba, "We're eyeball to eyeball and the other fellow just blinked." The question is: If we are ever at the brink again and the Soviet Union has the perceived military advantage, who will do the blinking? A country can be intimidated into accepting defeat. We must never forget that weakness is provocative, as history clearly records.

A while back Secretary of State Henry Kissinger raised this rhetorical question: "What in the name of God is superiority? What could the Soviet Union do with it?" The secretary went on to say that nuclear superiority is devoid of any operational meaning. If he is right, the trends I am discussing are meaningless—for in this event assured destruction has rendered superiority useless. But if this is so, Why is the Soviet Union investing so heavily not only in achieving nuclear superiority but also in increasing it?

In early 1945, when our GIs were pushing toward Germany, it surely must have been unthinkable to us that anyone would send millions of men, women, and children into gas chambers. But, as it turned out, it was not unthinkable to Hitler. Admittedly, the Soviet leaders are more rational than Hitler was. Still, when one considers the prospect of nuclear war, one needs to ask: How does that prospect look to the enemy, when contemplated in terms of *his* philosophy and *his* definition of morality?

Soviet leaders talk in terms of first strike, or so their doctrines and military writings indicate. In a recent study, Jeffrey Record states that the most salient features of Soviet doctrine are "the primacy of the offensive, the decisive role of nuclear weapons, the extraordinary emphasis on mass and surprise and rapid rates of advance."[3] While U.S. doctrine emphasizes deterrence, Soviet doctrine states that defensive operations are "a forced and temporary form of combat actions" and that "a side which only defends is inevitably doomed to defeat," to

---

[3] Jeffrey Record, *Sizing Up the Soviet Army* (Washington, D.C.: Brookings Institution, 1975), p. 33.

quote Soviet military expert V. Ye. Savkin.[4] Another Soviet military analyst, A. S. Sidorenko, states that to forgo the first strike is "absolutely inadmissible."[5]

Soviet doctrine and force structure are propelled not only toward the primacy of the offensive but also toward offensive operations whose major aim is to prevent an effective military defense on the part of the opponent through preemptive attack.

The day the Soviet Union can achieve these goals of strategic superiority may be our last as a truly free nation. It is the responsibility of the U.S. Congress to be sure that day does not arrive. That is why I am pointing out that the Soviet leadership might have intentions that we do not even contemplate. Any American defense posture that does not take into account the character of Soviet doctrine and force structure rests on very shaky and risky grounds.

If the Soviet Union believed that nuclear superiority were not usable, it would not be doubling its throw weight as well as increasing the accuracy of its nuclear delivery systems—thus quadrupling its advantage over us—with the deployment of four new ICBMs. And it surely would not be developing still more new ICBMs, even before it completes the deployment of the new missiles in current production.

Regardless of the SALT talks, the momentum of the Soviet buildup shows no sign of slackening. But, as the Soviet

---

[4] V. Ye. Savkin, *The Basic Principles of Operational Art and Tactics,* U.S. Air Force translation (Washington, D.C.: U.S. Government Printing Office, 1974), pp. 241-242.

[5] A. S. Sidorenko, *The Offensive,* U.S. Air Force translation (Washington, D.C.: U.S. Government Printing Office, 1973), p. 134.

buildup has continued, the United States has relied on SALT, and no new U.S. ICBM system has been developed.

Secretary of Defense Donald Rumsfeld testified before the House Appropriations Subcommittee on Defense, of which I am a member, that the trends of the past ten years "are adverse with respect to the military balance."[6] Some members of Congress disagree with him. More to the point, however, Soviet Foreign Minister Andrei Gromyko agrees with Secretary Rumsfeld's assessment. Interpreting the same trends, Mr. Gromyko stated last September in *Kommunist,* the monthly organ of the Communist Party of the Soviet Union, that the forces of international communism now have a "visibly increased preponderance" and may now be in a position "to lay down the direction of international politics."[7] Whether they are or are not in that position at this time, there is every indication that they intend to be there soon.

It is certainly in the interests of the American people, and in the interests of peace and freedom in the world, for us in the Congress to do our part to help prevent the Soviet leaders from achieving the position toward which they are driving. We must make it useless for them to try.

Not since the war preparations of Nazi Germany under Hitler in the 1930s has a major nation at peace devoted such a high percentage of its resources to the production of weapons and to the buildup of the related scientific, technical, and industrial base for military production. The sooner we in the

---

[6] U.S. Congress, House, Subcommittee on Defense of the Appropriations Committee, "FY 77 U.S. Defense Budget Perspectives," February 26, 1976.

[7] Quoted from *The Economist,* February 7, 1976, p. 9.

United States realize that the U.S.S.R. is engaged in a tremendous military buildup that will allow it to use nuclear blackmail and intimidation to "lay down the direction of international politics," the greater the chance for peace and freedom in the world.

If those people who view our own defense establishment with suspicion and yet see the Russian buildup through rose-colored glasses succeed in preventing us from upgrading our triad deterrent by blocking procurement of the B-1 bomber, the Trident, the Minuteman III, and the cruise missile, we will have greatly increased the risk of war to ourselves and our allies. Our interests will be respected only if Soviet leaders believe we can defend those interests. Restraint will prevail only if its absence means heavy risks. If we let our defense posture weaken, we will have indeed made the world safe for Communist imperialism.

I do not want to play the role of an alarmist, but there are many facts which need to be brought to the attention of the American people. These facts demonstrate the challenge that the tremendous Soviet weapons capability presents to our ability to maintain a high quality deterrent in the interest of the peace and freedom of the United States and our allies.

Turning to the area of conventional military forces, the question becomes, Which country is stronger in non-nuclear weapons? There is, unfortunately, only one answer to that question: the Soviet Union.

The growing superiority of Soviet conventional military power is described in Jeffrey Record's *Sizing Up the Soviet Army*. That study shows that Russian military forces have the capability and the mission of carrying out a "relentless attack, blitzkrieg style, designed to ensure the total defeat of the enemy. . . . The achievement of such unlimited goals in the case of a conflict in the European area would entail nothing short of a giant blitzkrieg across NATO Center leading to the rapid occupation of West Germany, the Low Countries, and France."[8] The author finds that the thirty-one combat-ready full-strength Russian divisions stationed in Eastern Europe "clearly reflect willful preparation for massive, rapid offensive operations at the theater level in Europe." They expect to be able to roll across NATO forces to the English Channel within a week.[9]

Record's study also gives depressing comparisons between Soviet and U.S. forces and recites the immense amount of money spent on modernizing the Soviet army. During 1972-1974, the Russians out-produced the United States by average annual ratios of 6½ to 1 in tanks, 5 to 1 in armored personnel carriers, and 7 to 1 in artillery pieces. By 1974 the United States had 2,600 medium tanks, while the U.S.S.R. had "a staggering 30,700."[10]

The study concludes that Soviet military doctrine is geared to the strategy of surprise attack, based on "massive shock power and speed; the former, to crush the enemy's initial defenses; the latter, to prevent recovery so that the enemy can be beaten in detail. . . . The Soviet Union attaches great importance to achieving both strategic and tactical surprise in future combat."[11]

[8] Record, *Sizing Up the Soviet Army,* p. 34 and p. 36.
[9] Ibid., p. 33 and p. 43.
[10] Ibid., p. 27.
[11] Ibid., p. 35 and p. 42.

The implications for NATO of this report are corroborated by a recent White Paper published by the West German government. This analysis finds: "Initiative and surprise occupy a place of paramount importance in the military strategic thinking of the Warsaw Pact. . . . A surprise attack could be launched by the Warsaw Pact with practically no preparation and without any build-up—from maneuver situations for instance. It could, in such an operation, exploit the advantages of the attacker and determine the time of the attack as well as its points of key effort."[12]

The evidence is inescapable: if we eliminate nuclear weapons from our calculations on the theory they will never be used, then Soviet military superiority over the United States is overwhelming.

The decline in the strength of our navy is perhaps an even more dramatic case in point. In the face of a major expansion of Soviet naval forces, one that has altered the character of the naval balance, the size of the U.S. fleet has diminished sharply. In fiscal year 1968 the U.S. Navy had 976 ships; this fiscal year the number will be only 483. The shrinkage reflects the disappearance from the fleet of vessels constructed during World War II, some thirty years ago, as well as the postponement of naval construction during the Vietnam War and the present lack of shipyard capacity. But our navy's commitments in the Far East and in the Mediterranean have

---

[12] Press and Information Office of the Government of the Federal Republic of Germany, *The Security of the Federal Republic of Germany and the Development of the Federal Armed Forces—White Paper 1975/1976* (Bonn: Federal Minister of Defense on Behalf of the Federal Government, 1976), p. 17.

not shrunk commensurately. As a result, today's smaller fleet is overworked in the attempt to maintain those commitments. The consequence has been a distressing decline in the material readiness of the fleet.

The decay in the condition of the U.S. fleet was dramatically underscored during the U.S. response to the Mayaguez incident. The thirty-one-year-old U.S.S. *Hancock,* which had been operating without one of its four shafts, limped belatedly from Subic Bay toward the Gulf of Thailand at twenty-three knots, but never reached the scene. The helicopter carrier U.S.S. *Okinawa,* with part of its boiler plant off the line, crept along at thirteen or fourteen knots; it also never arrived. The escort vessel U.S.S. *Holt,* the first ship at the scene, had power-supply problems and, consequently, its main battery was down the night before the engagement. Clearly, this nation cannot for long tolerate the present readiness condition of the U.S. Navy if it is to continue to rely on the navy for rapid response.

Since 1965 the Soviet navy has been altered in significant ways. Before then it had operated primarily as a coastal-defense and interdiction force. Now, with the introduction of more capable classes of ships, it has become a formidable blue-water navy presenting a first-strike challenge to the United States. Soviet fleets operate increasingly in the Indian Ocean, have begun to edge out the United States in the seas around Japan, and in certain respects have become a match for the U.S. Sixth Fleet in the Mediterranean, formerly an American lake.

Within the Soviet Union, the promise of detente has brought mostly rhetoric thus far, with virtually no results to the United States. In give-and-take, it is the Americans who are giving and the Russians who are taking. Soviet leaders and official propagandists have consistently made it clear that detente and coexistence require an intensification of the "ideological struggle"—which is to them a euphemism for export of, and support for, wars of "national liberation." In Leonid Brezhnev's words: "Peaceful co-existence . . . rests on a system of principles that make it possible to avoid a major international conflict in the course of development of revolutionary processes within individual countries. . . . Ideological struggle and cold war are totally different concepts."[13]

The struggle for "national liberation"—which Soviet policy actively discourages in Eastern Europe—is actively promoted and supported in other areas. Indeed, the Soviet Union described the Arab attacks on Israel as a "war of national liberation," and it has also justified its own use of surrogate Cuban troops in Angola on this basis. Any relaxation of ideological tensions has been explicitly rejected. In the Soviet Union and in most of its East European satellites as well, the official policy of normalizing relations with the United States has been the occasion for intensified political repression and for campaigns stressing the importance of the struggle against so-called reactionary forces and the victory of socialism in the world arena.

In the final analysis, the level of U.S. defense spending should not be decided on the basis of dollar-ruble comparisons

---

[13] Leonid Brezhnev, *Report of the Central Committee of the Communist Party of the Soviet Union to the Twenty-fifth Party Congress: Immediate Objectives of the Party in Domestic and Foreign Affairs,* February 24, 1976.

or the desire to create jobs. It should not be dictated by a comparison with the level of spending on domestic programs or by what we think it would be nice to have. Lastly, it must not be dictated by what anyone presumes Soviet intentions to be.

It must be decided on the basis of the actual Soviet military capability, regardless of the cost of that capability to the Soviet Union. It must be dictated by an understanding of the size and kind of forces that we might have to meet in a crisis. It must be dictated by conditions in the world over which we do not often have control.

It was only a few years ago that I heard members of Congress standing on the floor of the House of Representatives telling us that if we cut our defense spending dramatically, the Russians would cut theirs. I notice we do not hear much of that sort of rhetoric anymore.

It was only a few years ago that we frequently heard speakers on the floor of the House arguing that the United States had to refrain from developing new missile or aircraft systems because to develop these systems might endanger the conclusion of a SALT agreement. It was not so long ago that people told us we should avoid developing follow-on weapons systems because they too might endanger detente.

Well, we have a SALT agreement. But it has not stopped the Soviet Union from developing new and more powerful follow-on strategic systems. And I notice that the word detente is not even used anymore in some quarters.

We of all people should know that military power is not simply the sum total of all the soldiers, tanks, ships, aircraft, and missiles in the national inventory. The secret to our military successes has been the maintenance of technological and qualitative supremacy over our potential adversaries. And, as President John Kennedy said, in that race, there is no first or second, there is only first and last.

The highly regarded report of the Library of Congress on the U.S./Soviet military balance shows that the Soviet drive for supremacy will continue unless U.S. decision makers take determined steps to slow and then reverse current trends. "As it stands," the report concludes, "the quantitative balance continues to shift toward the Soviet Union. U.S. qualitative superiority never compensated completely and, in certain respects, is slowly slipping away." [14]

Recently we have had a level of healthy debate on the defense budget that is unprecedented for budget debates in this country. I have participated—as I know my friend, Les Aspin, has—and I believe it has been extremely useful. It is important to point out, however—against the backdrop of our debate—that there has been no public debate in the Soviet Union on the Soviet defense budget, and there is no visible dissent there. The size of the Russian military has been growing steadily and on an ominous scale. There have been no Soviet retrenchments, no distractions, no reordering of priorities as we know them. As former Secretary of Defense Melvin Laird said recently.

> The facts are that, in recent months, the U.S.S.R.— secretly and openly—has repeatedly committed deliberate acts that mock detente and threaten the

[14] Library of Congress, Congressional Research Service, *United States/Soviet Military Balance* (Washington, D.C.: U.S. Government Printing Office, 1976), p. 41.

free world. . . . Clearly, we must shed any lingering illusions we may have that the Russians have abandoned their determination to undermine Western democracy and impose their system upon the world.[15]

There can be—and there is—reasonable disagreement as to how specific and how great the Soviet threat is in any one area. Comparisons of military forces are complex. Honest differences of opinion exist over the reliability or relevance of the various indexes of military strength.

There is, however, no difference of opinion over the trends. The trends favor the Soviet Union, not the United States. The trends in the U.S./Soviet military balance are, in the aggregate, adverse to the U.S. national interest, and they must be arrested and reversed. In historical perspective there is only one thing worse than an arms race—and that is arms inferiority.

Today, our basic security position is strong, but, as I have pointed out, we must not ignore the adverse trends. Our fundamental national interest in world politics is to achieve and maintain a balance of power which can effectively deter war. If, with our allies, we do what is required to offset Soviet nuclear and conventional power, we should be able to carry out a foreign policy capable of preventing war, while also pressing forward diplomatically in our quest for peace. If, on the other hand, we allow ourselves to be deceived by a myth of detente, if we reduce our military strength and permit our alliances to erode, we may well suffer irreversible defeats,

[15] Melvin R. Laird, "Is this Detente?" *Reader's Digest,* July 1975, p. 54 and p. 57.

which could imperil freedom in America and peace for the world.

The challenge of defense policy for the United States is difficult, but manageable. We have the resources to do the job, if we arrive at a common understanding of the threat and of what is required to meet that threat.

SECOND LECTURE

LES ASPIN

I think the question of how much defense spending is enough is, indeed, an answerable question.

Let me begin by discussing spending for conventional forces, in order to expand the debate a little, inasmuch as Congressman Kemp focused his paper primarily on strategic forces. The conventional forces, or what are called the general-purpose forces, receive most of the money in the defense budget. About 80 percent of that budget is spent on conventional forces. How are we to decide how much is enough for the conventional forces?

When Secretary of Defense Robert McNamara first went to the Pentagon, he gave these instructions: "List every trouble spot in the world, suppose they all erupted at once, and then determine how many forces the United States would need to take care of itself in that kind of a situation." Well, the answer came back and the numbers were, of course, staggering: fifty or more divisions and mountains of equipment. So then he said, "We cannot assume that all the trouble spots in the world will erupt at once. What would happen if we assumed, instead, that only some of them erupted simultaneously?" Eventually, out of this exercise, we evolved what was called the two-and-a-half war strategy. This strategy assumed that two major contingencies could happen at once, along with one of the minor contingencies. Later, that was revised under Secretary Melvin Laird to a "one-and-a-half war strategy." The military, incidentally, has never been happy with that strategy. They argue that we never really had the forces to fight either two-and-a-half wars or one-and-a-half wars.

Nevertheless, the theory of how to go about planning for an adequate defense is, I think, still applicable. I think the way to determine how much defense spending is enough is, first, to look at the world posture of the United States and to ask what are the vital foreign interests that the United States must defend and what are our vital national security interests. From that, we can derive the force levels necessary to defend those areas.

I personally would maintain that, in addition to the North American continent, the areas that are of vital interest to the United States are Europe, Japan, and the Middle East. I would be doubtful of much beyond that. I think that there would be substantial agreement in the Congress that Japan, Europe, and the Middle East are the major areas of U.S. interest, but, beyond that, the agreement would break down.

If the question of defense spending levels were approached in this way, I think we could begin to arrive at an answer. It would not give us a single figure, accepted by all—obviously, there would be disagreements. There would be disagreements between Jack Kemp and myself as to what our vital interests are and what forces are necessary to defend them. But at least the debate would be rational. At least there would be some direction to the whole argument, and we could then proceed to think about ways to improve the efficiency of the Department of Defense. Once we had decided on the general force levels that were needed, we could then ask questions about efficiency, pensions, pay and allowances, et cetera.

That would be a rational way to go about producing a defense budget, and we would end up with a smaller budget than we have now. But, we do not go about it in that way. The question is, Why not? Obviously there are some institutional factors to prevent us from doing that. But there are two other factors as well that are particularly pertinent. Both relate to the climate in which we approach the Defense Department budget today, in 1976.

One is a crazy overreaction some people have to what the Soviet Union is doing with its defense budget. The debate seems to revolve around such questions as, Who spends more? Who has more equipment, tanks, planes, et cetera? What are the defense spending trends in the two countries? And how do the two countries compare in various combinations of these items?

Let me try to put this matter into perspective as I see it. First of all, the debate on who is spending more on defense, the Soviet Union or the United States, is not very fruitful. If the calculations are made in dollars, it turns out that the U.S.S.R. is spending more. If they are made in rubles, it turns out that the United States is spending more. Moreover, the debate on who has more equipment is also unfruitful. Clearly, the Soviet Union has a lot more of certain kinds of equipment than we have, but it faces certain rather special conditions.

First, the Soviet Union has an enemy on its border, China. Second, there is the quality factor. We have less equipment than the Soviet Union but of better quality. Third, historically the Soviet Union has had higher inventories. For some reason, it never throws anything away. The Soviet armed forces just keep piling stuff up in inventory—they are absolutely buggy

25

about equipment. For example, at the beginning of World War II, the Soviet Union had more tanks than all of the other countries in the world put together. It did not know how to use them, as the Germans did, and the tanks were not very good. But the Soviet Union has always had a lot of equipment.

The final factor in U.S. versus Soviet defense spending relates to trends, and here a point has to be made. I think it is true that the Soviet defense budget has been increasing steadily—but not very quickly—over the last ten years. During the same period, overall, the U.S. defense budget has been declining. It went up because of Vietnam until 1968 and then went down. But, from 1964 through 1974, eliminating the bulge for Vietnam, there was an overall 1 percent per year decline. The Soviet defense budget, on the other hand, increased 2.5 percent to 3 percent per year in that period.

These trends obviously cannot be ignored. They are a matter for concern, and they raise many interesting questions about what the Soviet leaders are doing. But the trends should not dissuade us from rational decision making on defense spending, and they especially should not panic us into increasing our defense budget astronomically. But, unfortunately, that seems to be what we are doing.

The other factor, besides Soviet defense spending, that prevents us from having a rational debate about defense is that we are wrapped up in what may be called the credibility complex. It is an outgrowth of Vietnam and Watergate. It arises because a rather large number of people, abroad as well as in this country, think that neither the people nor the government of the United States has the will, the determination, and the unity of purpose to pursue its own self-interest and the interest of peace in the world. That is the credibility problem: we lack credibility in the world—or, at least, the people who conduct our foreign policy believe we lack credibility with our allies and our adversaries abroad.

International credibility is elusive. It was in pursuit of international credibility that we stayed in the war in Vietnam much longer than we should have. Other rational reasons for staying in the war had disappeared, but we stayed because of credibility. We were there initially to fight for freedom; we were there to prevent aggression; we were there because of the domino theory; we were there because it was another Munich. All of those reasons, sooner or later, fell by the wayside. The reason we stayed, ultimately, was that, if we pulled out and abandoned that ally, our other allies around the world would think that we would abandon them, too, when things got tough. It is this concern for credibility that prevents us from rationally determining our national security interests.

We ought to go back and redefine our defense posture on Japan, Western Europe, and the Middle East, because our vital interests lie in these areas. But we are committed to many more countries around the world—forty-four countries, in fact—and we have "informal agreements," as Kissinger says, with dozens more. We have commitments to two-thirds of the countries in the world.

The reason we do not rearrange the alliance structure is credibility. After Watergate, after Vietnam, we fear we cannot rearrange our alliances without losing more credibility. It is this fear that propels us into places where we do not have any commitments, like Angola.

In the debate over how much the Soviet Union is spending on defense, I think the credibility point is not total nonsense. It is real. Ultimately it is related to the nuclear deterrent, for the nuclear deterrent rests on credibility. The only way we can be sure we will never have to use nuclear weapons is if our adversaries find it credible that we might use them.

Credibility spills over into arguments for greater defense budgets. Many people appear to think that, just for credibility's sake, we ought to have a bigger defense budget—that, somehow, increasing the defense budget will increase our credibility in the world, no matter how the money is spent. I think they are wrong. Credibility cannot be purchased with greater spending on defense. Even if we doubled the defense budget, we would not restore U.S. credibility to the level of the late 1950s and early 1960s, before Vietnam.

On the other hand, it is possible that the defense budget cannot be cut very much. A very large cut in the defense budget might well damage credibility. Indeed, there may be some asymmetry there.

These two factors—the concern over what the Russians are spending on defense and the concern over credibility—are preventing us from having a rational defense budget, one that could be much smaller than the present one.

My answer to how much is enough consists of two parts, a recommendation for this year's defense budget and a recommendation for the long run. As for the current defense budget, I think we ought to cut to the President's request. The President is proposing a 7 percent real increase for defense spending, but I think, in the short run, we should have a 2 percent real increase. Given what the Russians are doing, there is an argument for a real increase in the defense budget. Let us match the Soviet Union's increase while we figure out what to do. We can match the Soviet Union's real increase and still cut the President's request.

Such a cut is important because there is too much in that budget which the Pentagon officials did not think would survive congressional scrutiny. When they made up this budget, they had no idea that Congress would be in a mood to pass everything they sent over this year. They produced their usual budget request, with a lot of "cut insurance," a lot of fat that they expected Congress to cut out. If they were making up that budget today, they would do it very differently. In my view, there is room to cut, and if we do not cut, we will have to make a record number of reprogramming decisions in the next Congress.

In the long run, we really have to think through the question of what the Russians are spending and what our response ought to be. We ought to think through the question of credibility, and whether credibility is indivisible. If we lose credibility in Angola, does that reflect on the credibility of our nuclear deterrent? I think we must seek answers to this sort of question.

Ultimately we arrive at the problem that the kind of forces we buy for the sake of perceptions are not the kind of forces we might buy for fighting a war. In the interest of perceptions of credibility, we would buy certain kinds of forces, such as aircraft carriers, that would not buy much readiness of the sort precision-guided munitions or captor mines would provide. When *U.S. News and World Report* publishes charts comparing U.S. and Soviet equipment, captor mines are not included, nor are laser-guided artillery shells or smart bombs. The focus is entirely upon tanks, armed personnel carriers, and similar equipment.

The debate is pushing us into higher defense budgets for the sake of higher defense budgets, and more numbers for the sake of more numbers. Perhaps these are not what we should be buying. Right now the concern about credibility and the concern about Russian spending are bedeviling the budget-cutters in Congress. But these two concerns will ultimately bedevil the people who are interested primarily in a strong and adequate United States.

REBUTTALS

JACK KEMP

I strongly agree with my friend and colleague, Les Aspin, that a healthy rational debate can bring about the paring, the reductions in manpower costs, and the increased efficiency that are needed in our defense program. In fact, he and I cooperated in attempting to remove a 1 percent kicker from the cost of living increase in military personnel retirement pay. That action would have saved $1 billion over the next three to four years. We have failed so far because the Congress has not been willing to remove a similar 1 percent kicker from civil service retirement, which would have saved another $1 billion.

So the healthy debate this country needs has begun—and this meeting is part of it.

Let me note that the trends my friend from Wisconsin alluded to in his opening remarks are much more ominous that he seems to think. There is, we must remember, no such healthy debate on priorities going on in the Soviet Union, at least not in public. As I have said, the question of how much is enough is not a question of dollars versus rubles or equipment versus equipment. It is, rather, a question of perceptions. It is a question, indeed, of credibility, and it is a question of which side would blink if we should ever again reach the brink, as we did during the 1962 Cuban missile crisis.

Former Secretary of State Dean Rusk said that the Soviet Union blinked in 1962 primarily because of the credibility of our deterrent, because of our strategic superiority. The question is, Who would blink today if we were to come to that brink again? But even more worrisome is what might happen in 1980, 1981, 1982. I think there has to be some question about which side would blink in the early 1980s if steps are not taken to reverse these present trends.

The purpose of spending more money to increase the real growth in the defense budget by 7 percent, following the last few years of cuts, is to upgrade our deterrent, primarily our triad, which consists of land-based and sea-based intercontinental ballistic missiles as well as the intercontinental bomber force. An increase in the real growth of the U.S. defense budget would send a strong diplomatic signal to the Soviet Union. It would say that we want to reduce the arms race, that we are willing to negotiate, but that negotiations must be on a mutual, reciprocal, quid pro quo basis, and, in the absence of Soviet willingness to negotiate honestly and in good faith, we will take the steps necessary to upgrade our deterrent capability.

What I am talking about is trends. I am concerned that, by the 1980s—when the Soviet Union will be bringing on line a new generation of sea- and land-based intercontinental ballistic missiles, having already built a massive military capability in both conventional and strategic terms—this nation could be facing the Soviet Union in a diplomatic crisis. There is doubt in the minds of some very able and dedicated people as to which side would blink in those circumstances.

I agree with my friend that we should spend money only for the vital national security interests of this country. I am not interested, as some might be, in the United States' being a policeman for the world. But we must remind ourselves that the Soviet Union certainly is not a policeman, and that the world is a dangerous place today—certainly more dangerous than it was a few years ago. This becomes very clear, it seems to me, if we look at the military trends—defense spending, the nature of the Soviet buildup—and at what has happened in Angola and in the rest of Africa.

Angola in and of itself is not what is at stake. The answer to what happened in Angola was not to be found in Luanda. The answer, it seems to me, was to be found in Moscow. And for the United States to send a signal to Moscow that we were willing to negotiate SALT II—to send our secretary of state to Moscow—at a time when the Soviet Union was supporting and exporting Cuban revolutionary forces in Angola was the wrong kind of signal to send.

I believe that in the absence of a sound SALT II agreement, current world conditions require that this nation take strong steps to upgrade its strategic and conventional military capability.

LES ASPIN

Let me begin by mentioning something that Congressman Kemp alluded to—and I have heard others say it as well, particularly in the Pentagon. I am referring to the statement that the military buildup in the Soviet Union is the greatest since Hitler's in World War II. That is absolutely crazy. The implication is that the Russians are building up a massive force in an attempt to catch us off guard and to annihilate the United States.

It is possible that they are doing it by incremental steps, but if they are, they are not doing it very seriously. A 2.7 percent increase per year is what the Soviet Union has had. To say that that is the biggest increase since Germany's under Hitler is absurd when you look at the last ten years. In that period the Chinese defense budget was increased by 8 percent per year, the Japanese defense budget by 9 percent per year, and the Israeli defense budget by over 20 percent per year. The Soviet Union has not had the largest increase in defense expenditures since Hitler's in World War II.

What are the Soviet leaders up to? Are they really out to do us in? Maybe—maybe not. My guess is probably not. In my judgment, what is going on in the Soviet Union has a lot more to do with the fact that they are Russians than with the fact that they are Communists. I believe that the Russians are committed to a philosophy which leads to certain kinds of results. There is a paranoia in the Soviet Union about defense.

37

They always think that they are under attack. They have an ideology that tells them that history is with them and that they must take advantage of opportunity.

I think that some of what the Soviet leaders do, perhaps, is done for internal reasons. But what is clear is that they move in increments. They have no really sophisticated view, of the kind Congressman Kemp was saying we have, on how much is enough. They probably figure that, in general, a little bit more is better than a little bit less. Moreover, they take advantage of things that come along. There is no question that they will take advantage of the Angolas that come along.

However, to say that the Soviet Union will exploit targets of opportunity is not to say that it is building a defense establishment that is getting ready, preparing secretly and quietly, for war with the United States.

It is my judgment that the Soviet leadership realizes the dangers of nuclear war. I think that it realizes more than most countries what warfare really means. Judgments of this kind are obviously something we have to be careful about. Miscalculations can occur. Of course a war is possible between the two countries. But I do not think we can look at what the Soviet Union is doing and conclude that it is building up to try a deliberate attack on the United States, which is what this Hitler analogy seems to suggest.

So what do we do about it? We have several options, and I am really not sure which is best for us. We could match them, that is, if they are increasing their defense budget by X percent, we could increase ours by X percent. Second, we could, perhaps, open negotiations with them on the totality of the defense budget. Or, third, we could let it be known to them—through diplomatic, as well as through open public channels—that we know their defense budget is increasing, and that we are very unhappy about it. In fact, we have already done the third, and it has already been noted—as various people who watch the Soviet press have reported.

I think there is a very great danger that our response could be an over-response.

Our whole history of dealing with the Soviet Union seems to be one of oscillations between extremes. They were our good friends in World War II and right after SALT. They were our worst enemies after World War II and are again today. Let us not have these oscillations. Let us have a more rational and a more consistent view of Soviet objectives and actions: we must keep our eye on them, but we must understand that they are not out to commit suicide.

DISCUSSION

JOHN CHARLES DALY, former ABC News executive and moderator of the debate: Congressman Aspin and Congressman Kemp have concluded their rebuttals and are now ready to take questions from the many experts in the audience.

ROBERT SHERMAN, staff, office of Representative Thomas J. Downey (Democrat, New York): My question is directed at both Congressman Aspin and Congressman Kemp. Considering the great concern we have now over the growing Soviet counterforce capability, and considering that the U.S.S.R. did not have MIRVs when the first SALT talks began, do you believe we made a mistake by not going for a MIRV ban back then when we could have gotten it? And are we making a mistake now by not going for a MARV [multiple automatically targeted reentry vehicles] ban, which we could get now but would not be able to get four or five years after it has been tested?

MR. ASPIN: A brief answer—yes. I believe we did make a mistake by not trying to get a MIRV ban in SALT I, and I think that it would be a mistake not to try to get a MARV ban in SALT II.

MR. KEMP: I think the assumption upon which the question is based is false. That assumption is that we could have gotten a MIRV ban at SALT I and now could get a MARV ban at SALT II.

Of course, we ought to reduce the numbers of warheads and the amount of throw weight and megatonnage in any new agreement. But we are ignoring recent historical experience with the Soviet negotiating postures at SALT if we assume that: (1) We could have had, at SALT I, the kind of agreement the gentleman described in his question; and (2) even if we had gotten it, it would have been kept by the Soviet Union, which has pushed every ambiguity and every possible loophole in SALT I, and in the Vladivostok agreement, to the limit.

JAMES HESSMAN, *Seapower Magazine*: Alexander Solzhenitsyn has said, looking at the map of the world in 1945 and today, that World War III has been fought and that the Soviet Union has won. I would like to ask each of the panelists to comment on this statement and on what it implies for the future.

MR. KEMP: Alexander Solzhenitsyn has one of the most unique perspectives of an individual on the face of this earth. I, personally, see him as one of the world's greatest and most powerful spokesmen, not only for western civilization, but also for the independence and freedom of all people.

Whether or not, semantically, we choose to describe the condition in which we are currently engaged with the Soviet Union as World War III is not as important as some of the things talked about earlier: the current trends and the willingness of the Soviet Union to devote such a major proportion of its gross national product to militarism. The burden that it is willing to assume in order to achieve strategic and nuclear superiority, as well as conventional superiority, could, at some point in the near future, put this nation in a position where, in the event of a diplomatic crisis like the Cuban missile crisis, it would be the United States that would have to give in on a vital national interest.

I would also point to the recent past, the Yom Kippur War of October 1973, when the United States received strong signals from Moscow that the Soviet Union would march troops into the Persian Gulf if we allowed the Israelis to capture the Third Egyptian Army. Now this nation depends upon Persian Gulf oil for about 20 percent of its industrial fuel; Europe's dependency is something like 75 or 80 percent and Japan's perhaps 70 percent.

It seems to me that, with vital interests of the United States around the world at stake, it does not behoove us to do anything less than everything possible to upgrade our strategic and conventional capabilities.

MR. ASPIN: To answer the gentleman's question about Solzhenitsyn, I think Solzhenitsyn is a very great man—and, like a lot of great men, he is prone to exaggeration.

JOSEPH THACH, Department of Defense: My question is for either or both congressmen.

A number of recent authors have come out with a general scenario for Europe involving two phases: first, conventional war, during which the Soviet Union would rapidly overrun Western Europe, and then the use of nuclear blackmail to frighten the United States into not doing anything about it. How do we go about accomplishing a trade-off between general-purpose forces and strategic forces in order to prepare for that possible contingency?

MR. ASPIN: You are talking just of the context of Europe?

MR. THACH: Primarily.

MR. ASPIN: I think we ought to have a sufficient conventional force to deter the Soviet Union from a conventional attack. That is critical to the European balance. Indeed, I would increase spending for some aspects of conventional forces. I would increase spending in the areas of readiness, primarily, and in the areas that fall between the various service interests or subservice interests: for example, some kinds of precision-guided munitions, captor mines, communications equipment (which tends to get lost in the shuffle because neither the submariners nor the air or surface navy is all that interested in it), and things like that.

In other words, I would say that if I were concerned about any balances, I would be much more concerned about the conventional balance than I am about the strategic balance.

MR. KEMP: I do not disagree at all with my colleague's references to the need to expand the capability of our conventional forces. Indeed, I applaud his remarks.

I think I have made clear in this debate my feelings about what we need to do in the case of our strategic capability. I also think that much more needs to be done with regard to our allies in NATO, whose southern flank is in danger.

I would go back to his earlier statement, with which I strongly concur: credibility is the United States' first line of defense. And I think that our credibility requires that steps be taken now. I think that the current defense budget, the proposed defense budget for fiscal year 1977, sends a strong signal, if you will, not only to Moscow but also to other capitals of the world, that this nation will do what is necessary to upgrade its strategic and conventional capabilities. I would continue that process, and I would do whatever else we can to assure our NATO allies that we will cooperate, that we will give them the help and assurances that are necessary, and that we will require of them increasing defense expenditures on their own behalf as well.

ROB OATES, staff, office of Representative Steve Symms (Republican, Idaho): My question is for Congressman Aspin. Dr. Kissinger's policy for slowing what he has termed the "inevitable decline" of the United States as a world power has seriously lessened our influence around the world, and many observers even believe now that the United States would lose in a nuclear showdown with the Soviet Union. The Soviet leadership continually reiterates its long-term goal of world domination. Recent examples of this have been the events in the Middle East and in Angola. In view of its actions, how can you justify ignoring its often stated goal of world domination?

MR. ASPIN: I do not ignore it. I think the Soviet leaders would like to dominate the world—as would a lot of other countries—but they will not be able to do it, and they are not going to commit suicide in an attempt to do it. So we must make sure that they are not able to do it.

There have been all kinds of ideologies in the history of the world that have had world domination in mind. Islam and various other religions were going to dominate the world, but none of them was able to accomplish it. Eventually reality set in, and they adjusted to the real world. I do not believe for a minute that the Soviet Union is going to change its ideology or give up its rhetoric. Nor, for that matter, is the United States. There is a lot of rhetoric associated with our country too, but reality forces us to act other than we would like in a lot of cases, just as reality has forced the Soviet Union to do things other than it would like. I think reality will continue to have that result. One purpose of the whole debate over how much defense is enough is to see to it that, even though Moscow might try to dominate the world, it could not succeed.

MR. KEMP: It is not enough to ask the rhetorical question, What is the Soviet Union up to? Nor is it enough, perhaps, to make predictions on the basis of past Soviet actions. It seems to me we ought to look at the real world. We need to look at the events that occurred in Southeast Asia following the signing of the Paris peace accords in January 1973—accords which the U.S.S.R. was to help guarantee along with the United States, but did not. We ought to look at the Middle East, or at Africa, where the U.S.S.R. is attempting to imperialize and to establish bases in Somalia, in Angola, or perhaps even in Mozambique. In addition, we should take notice of the vast Soviet naval buildup, which has enlarged the Soviet navy from a conventional force with a mere defense capability to a blue-water navy with a first-strike capability around the world.

It seems to me that, given those real world examples, the United States ought to take very seriously the need to upgrade both parts of its military capability. I think it is setting up straw men to suggest that the U.S.S.R. is only attempting to overthrow the United States. I have never made that statement, and I do not think it will happen, certainly not with our current strategic and conventional forces deployed.

The question is—and I have raised this question a number of times—what will happen by the early 1980s if we do not upgrade our triad and if we continue to accommodate Soviet interests? The Soviet leaders are rational men, as was Adolf Hitler when he denied help to Mussolini in 1936 when fascist Italy moved into Abyssinia in northern Africa. Hitler would not help fascist Italy because of his concern that, if he did, the Western allies would rise up, close the Suez Canal, and begin to rearm. He did not want to give them a signal. No one in the West moved. Hitler's next step was to massively rearm Germany. The next step was to move into the Rhineland, then Austria, the Sudetenland, Czechoslovakia, and, ultimately, Poland, starting World War II. What I am suggesting is that a continual accommodation of American foreign policy to Soviet interests and moves, whether they are in Africa, the Middle East, or anywhere else in the world, seems likely to bring on a condition in which there will not be a chance for peace in the world.

MR. ASPIN: Let me just expand a bit more, because I think we are on an interesting question. If we look at what has happened in the last ten years to the standing of the United States and to the standing of the Soviet Union, I think we have to say that this has not been a great period for either of the superpowers. Both have suffered some setbacks. The United States obviously has, most particularly in Southeast Asia. But I think, on balance, the last ten years have been worse for the Soviet Union than for the United States.

We tend to emphasize whatever is going on—for example, recent events in Angola, Soviet inroads into southern Africa, and maybe the Italian elections. And we look on these things as being favorable to the Soviet Union.

But if we look more carefully at what has happened over the last ten to twelve years, we have to conclude that these have been very tough times for the Soviet Union. First, the Soviet Union lost its best ally, China. Until then we all had assumed that any war with Russia meant a war with China too. We cannot make that assumption anymore. In fact, the most likely war right now is a war between China and Russia. Second, the Soviet Union has had a miserable policy in the Middle East. The Russians have become everybody's enemy. It is incredible how they could have loused that up so badly. Third, the Soviet Union is now dependent upon the United States for, of all things, wheat.

Now, let us examine those three developments. Suppose they had happened to the United States. Suppose that the United States had lost its greatest ally—in other words, suppose that in the last ten years Western Europe had become an enemy. Suppose we had been expelled from the Middle East. And suppose we had become dependent upon the Soviet Union for wheat. Can you imagine the uproar that would be heard in this country about what was happening to the trends and how the Soviet Union was getting stronger and we were getting weaker?

And I have not mentioned a lot of other developments: Romania is moving toward greater independence. The Soviet Union and the Communists botched up their chance to do something in Portugal. Southeast Asia has thrown the United States out, but that does not mean it has moved into the Soviet orbit. And even half-crazed Cambodia has not ended up in the Soviet orbit.

The last ten years have not been very good for the Soviet Union, though there are a couple of instances of Soviet successes. I think Angola, Southern Africa, has been a success. But the U.S.S.R. has blundered in a lot of places and, on balance, it has come out of the last decade a lot worse than we have.

MR. KEMP: I would agree with Les. The Soviet leaders are not ten feet tall. They have made mistakes, and they continue to make mistakes. And there have been steps backward. A number of generations ago Lenin talked about taking one step backward in order to be able to take two or three forward. They are not ten feet tall.

But to suggest that the Soviet Union is worse off today vis-à-vis the United States than it was ten years ago, to suggest that the last ten years have been a disaster for the Soviet Union, is patently absurd and totally inconsistent with recent experience and with the events of the real world.

I do not want to sound like a broken record, but the Soviet buildup in strategic nuclear capability is incredible, whether you look at the present or two years hence or five years hence. Just taking land-based intercontinental ballistic warheads into account, the Soviet Union is MIRVing their new generation of launchers, thereby increasing the number of warheads from 1,600 to 8,400. They are also developing a mobile ICBM. This nation is so far away from any mobile-launched intercontinental ballistic missile that it is incredible. We are years away from any advanced warheads such as the MX, and we are light-years—no, that is too strong, we are a number of years—away from the type of advanced warhead for Minuteman III that most of us think ought to be developed.

The question, it seems to me, is the purpose and influence of the Soviet Union in the world today. Just take the matter of the establishment of Soviet hegemony over Eastern Europe that was codified at Helsinki in August 1975 and the other things that happened there. For the first time, this nation turned its back on the commitment to freedom and independence that has been the foundation of its foreign policy since World War II.

The SALT agreement, which originally was set up on the basis of giving this nation qualitative superiority in weapons, while giving the Soviet Union quantitative superiority, now is in danger. As I have already noted, the Library of Congress has warned that we are in danger of losing qualitative superiority by letting it slip away.

Again the question today is not just what has happened in the last ten years, but where this nation will be in terms of its foreign policy, and its interest in peace and freedom for itself and its allies, by the early 1980s. That is what the Congress has to take into consideration—not the existential moment in which we currently exist, but what type of world it is going to be for those who come after us.

GREGORY RUSHFORD, staff, former Intelligence Committee of the House of Representatives: There has been much confusion lately over whether the Soviet Union is complying with the provisions of the SALT agreement. Former Defense Secretary Laird and other high officials have alleged that the Russians are not negotiating in good faith and have not lived up to the terms and the spirit of, at least, the 1972 SALT accords. Can either of the panelists offer anything to clarify the situation?

MR. ASPIN: I think that basically the Soviet Union has not—and I emphasize *has not*—violated the SALT accords in any substantive way. Soviet leaders are, of course, going to take advantage of any ambiguities that exist in the accords. And there are, to be sure, a lot of ambiguities for them to take advantage of. Indeed, there are a lot of misperceptions about what the accords mean and what they do not mean among congressmen and the general public, thanks to the overselling of the accords by the administration.

But, when you come right down to it, has the Soviet Union substantially violated the SALT agreements? The answer, I think, is no. If we were to take it to a court of law, my honest opinion is that the answer would be no.

Now, to be sure, "They're going down the hotel corridor trying every door," to borrow that marvelous phrase by Senator Jackson. But they have not substantially violated the accord, and the inadvertent, unverified, or insubstantial violations which have occurred are matched by similar, and what I would consider insubstantial, violations on our part.

MR. KEMP: I find incredible the statement that Soviet violations of SALT are matched by those of the United States.

One need only look at our strategic nuclear position today, compared with what it was in 1968 and 1969 when the SALT talks began, to understand that Moscow has pushed ambiguities and nuances and loopholes to the absolute ultimate limits. I would agree with my friend that SALT was oversold. I would agree with my friend that we ought not to make an agreement until every *i* is dotted and every *t* crossed. And, to the extent that this nation has not pushed in the verification panel for on-site inspection, for verification, for consistency with the terms of the agreement, we are the losers and we are at fault rather than our adversaries.

SALT was, indeed, oversold in the beginning, and that was a mistake. I would agree that the violations to which the Soviet leaders have admitted—for example, just a few weeks ago they admitted they had not dismantled their SS-7s and SS-8s when they deployed delta-class nuclear subs—I would agree that violation is not as substantial as, perhaps, some people claim.

But what is serious is the extent to which we are willing to accept this kind of thing—so casually, so cavalierly. We are willing to accept, for instance, their replacing the SS-11 light intercontinental ballistic missile, which they had two or three years ago, with the SS-19, which we at one time considered a heavy missile. Now Secretary of State Kissinger tells us that the SS-19 is indeed not a heavy missile, even though it is 50 percent bigger than the SS-11 that it replaces. We now accept the SS-19 as a light missile, in total opposition to our understanding of a few years ago. We are also now willing to accept the construction of new concealed silos with blast-away covers—which the Russians call command-and-control centers—thus allowing the U.S.S.R. to increase its silos by 100 to 150.

There are several problem areas that ought to point out to the United States that we are not pushing hard enough in the verification process, that we ought to be much more careful as we enter into any further negotiations, if that is possible, involving the Vladivostok understandings. We need to recognize how serious it is for us to negotiate from anything less than a basis of complete reciprocity. I would suggest that those conditions have not been present, based upon the evidence that I have seen in the last few years of the SALT negotiations.

MR. ASPIN: I think that some of the examples that Congressman Kemp gave are examples of the confusion on our part. The Russians never agreed to our definitions of a light missile and heavy missile. We made a unilateral statement defining light and heavy missiles, and Congress was led to believe, by testimony from the administration, that the Russians were accepting this definition. But, in fact, they never did. So, if they never accepted it, they have not broken the accords on this count.

In other instances when we have protested, they have stopped. I think there will be more of those kinds of instances. This is a big world. Both sides have big bureaucracies, and things happen in one part of a country that the other parts of the country do not know are happening.

The case where we violated the accord was on covers of the Minuteman silos. The agreement specifically forbids covers on silos so that the other side can see what is going on. Out in North Dakota the technicians were working on the Minuteman silos. When it got cold, they put covers up because they wanted to keep warm and to harden the cement, and, in doing so, they happened to be in violation of the SALT accords. Eventually the violation was called to our attention, and we took the covers off.

Those kinds of incidents will continue to occur. I do not say that, in the Russians' case, all of the incidents are that innocent, but the Russians have backed off when we protested. As I said, I do not think any impartial court of law would find that the Russians have violated the accords.

MR. KEMP: In the absence of any impartial court of law to help us resolve the differences that now occur over SALT I, and in the absence of any international court of law to help resolve a conflict that might come about with the Soviet Union at some future time, and in the absence of any rational and credible court of law to help resolve the dispute if the Soviet Union should ever achieve the type of nuclear superiority that I have repeatedly suggested today they are attempting to achieve—in the absence of such a tribunal, it seems to me that it ought to be this nation's purpose, in our current defense budget and into the late 1970s, to make sure that we negotiate from a position of strength, that we insist on total mutuality and an absolute ability to verify. We should beware of an agreement like the one we entered into in SALT I, which left so many ambiguities and loopholes.

I would, also, take it one step further, Les. It seems to me that, with the Soviet Union pushing the SALT I accords to the limits, seeking every possible advantage and exploiting all loopholes, we ought to be very much on guard in the next round of SALT, when we try to negotiate an agreement on cruise missiles. I doubt that it would be verifiable except through on-site inspection—and that seems very difficult to bring about. I cannot recall many agreements that the Soviet Union has made a good faith effort to keep. I am deeply concerned about that as a member of Congress—directly responsible, as we are, to the people that we represent.

56

I just want to put the Russians on notice that I am one member of Congress who is going to make sure that the SALT agreement entered into by our secretary of state will be rigidly examined from two points of view: first, in regard to the capabilities it gives to the United States and the Soviet Union in terms of both quantity and quality, and, second, whether it is totally verifiable.

MR. ASPIN: I do not want to belabor the subject, but I want to agree with you on that point and also to say that I think it spells bad news for the SALT II negotiations— because obtaining cruise missile verification is clearly going to be a problem. We may end up with an agreement that will allow the Russians to cheat a little bit, but will allow us to be fairly confident, very confident, or even extremely confident that we can detect massive cheating on the Russian side. The question is, Will that kind of agreement be suitable to the Congress in the current climate, given the fact that the SALT I agreements have been oversold? My guess is that it will not, and that means big trouble because of the attitude that Jack Kemp says is very strong in Congress. The Congress is going to want everything spelled out in detail.

So, the reason we have not yet reached a SALT II agreement seems to be, first, the political reason that there is no constituency for SALT and the President is running for reelection, plus the fact that the kind of agreement that can be reached now will probably permit verification of massive violations but not of slight violations. That is the big, big trouble.

MR. DALY: For those of us who are wandering around in the thicket, would you explain what it is about the cruise missile that makes verification so difficult.

MR. KEMP: It is a pilotless, self-propelled guided bomb which can carry a nuclear warhead and is subsonic. It is very accurate, and it is inexpensive. Of course, there is a defense against it. But the massive numbers that could be built at a low cost would give a tremendous advantage to any nation that had both the accuracy that we have—that is, the technological leads in cruise missile hardware—and the ability to produce it in large numbers.

I would like to add this thought: it is not the climate in the Congress that has caused the breakdown in the SALT II negotiations, as far as I'm concerned. It is the willingness of the Congress, the willingness of the West, the willingness of our political leaders, both Democrat and Republican, to take a hard look at what has happened to the U.S.–U.S.S.R. balance in the last few years, and also to look at the U.S.S.R.'s willingness, or lack of it, to keep the agreements we have entered into with them in the past. I would emphasize again what happened after Helsinki. Does anyone in this room or anyone in the viewing audience really believe that the Soviet Union has done anything but massively violate the spirit, if not the letter of the law, of the Helsinki agreement? Within a few months, Moscow refused to allow physicist Andre Sakharov, the great Nobel Peace Prize winner, to go to Stockholm to receive his award. The U.S.S.R. was a coguarantor, as I mentioned earlier, of the Paris Peace Agreement. It also supported the Egyptian-Syrian attack on Israel during the Yom Kippur War, backed the oil embargo, and attempted at least rhetorically to deny the whole spirit of the Nixon-Brezhnev agreement reached in Moscow in 1972. I think the breakdown has resulted from the Soviet side rather than from some type of a climate in the U.S. Congress.

CHESTER EARLE, American University: I would like to ask each of the panelists for his overall position on the reported fact that the Soviet Union has been preparing elaborate logistical plans to evacuate large populations, whereas we evidently have no such plans. Would you comment on this and relate it to our civil defense posture and our willingness to think about the unthinkable?

MR. KEMP: I think I pointed out in my earlier remarks that the Soviet leaders *are* thinking about the unthinkable. That is one of the very strong factors that has to be taken into account in judging how much is enough. The Russians are thinking of the unthinkable, both in their military buildup and in their willingness to disperse industry, to build hardened sites, and to have massive civil defense procedures.

There are those in the Congress who say that all this is propaganda on Moscow's part, that it is cosmetic, that it is only an attempt to intimidate the West. Nonetheless, everybody who has visited Moscow recently sees in the subway, in the various areas of public ingress and egress, signs for civil defense.

There have been massive civil defense exercises—I say massive because entire cities have been emptied. The leaders of the Soviet Union are willing, as you point out, to think about the unthinkable in terms of this type of war survival mode.

In the 1950s, there apparently was a massive civil defense effort in Soviet Russia. In the 1960s, the Russians, like the Americans, gave up on this effort. There is evidence today— do not think it is just propaganda—to suggest they are once again attempting to upgrade considerably their war-survival effort. I think that should give us cause for concern.

MR. ASPIN: This whole debate seems to be about to become a discussion of the civil defense "gap"—and, as with all these gaps, there is something to it. But there is a very high percentage of nonsense about it, too. The Soviet Union does have some civil defense plans, and I guess we are going to have to look into it and figure out what they are up to.

The problem is that most of the claims have been made by people who want to increase our spending on civil defense and have been based upon Soviet manuals and other propagandistic materials. They claim, for example, that they can evacuate nearly everyone and achieve 90 percent survivability in a nuclear exchange.

I do not think anybody who has really studied this matter thinks the Soviet Union has that capability. If the Russians are that interested in civil defense, we ought to try to find out what they are actually doing.

My guess is that the debate on this issue is going to heat up, and obviously we shall have to look at the matter carefully to find out what is going on. But I do not think we ought, at this time, to believe a lot of rhetoric about what the Soviet Union is doing in the way of evacuation.

STUART LEVITAN, *Madison Capital Times*: I have two questions for Congressman Kemp. First, you mentioned America's interest in preserving peace and freedom around the world. I wonder how you reconcile that with your foreign policy position, which is based, in part, on associations and sometimes full treaties with some of the twentieth century's most repressive dictatorships? Second, do you feel we should have a first-strike capability doctrine?

MR. KEMP: Thank you so much for your questions. As to the first question, I definitely do not share the premise upon which it is based—namely, that we are committed to defending the most severely repressive nations on the face of the earth. This nation has made it quite clear, in many different ways for 200 years, that it is attempting to deter war by its conventional and strategic capability. Despite some mistakes, which there obviously are in any nation's history, this nation has a record that goes beyond that of any other in the history of mankind of making sacrifices in behalf of the freedom and peace of ourselves and our allies. It is far from perfect but— by any stretch of the imagination, by any relative real world standard—it seems to me that the United States has been a defender rather than an aggressor.

As to your second question about a first-strike capability, the question is academic. We do not have that capability. Our whole deterrent strategy is predicated upon our ability to retaliate against a first strike. And I am suggesting that the level of our defense spending should be determined on the basis of the actual Soviet buildup in conventional and strategic weapons and of the requirements for providing an effective deterrent to war, so on that I rest my case.

BRUCE STANLEY, Middle East Resource Center: I am interested that, in this discussion of how much defense spending is enough, the panelists have not even mentioned the relationship of defense spending to humanitarian concerns.

What does the fact that you do not put this question into a long-range, overall view of human development tell us about

61

the focus of this country? Why do you not put this question in the broader context?

MR. ASPIN: I think the reason that it has not been put into a broader context is not because we're not interested in humanitarian concerns or in programs that might lend assistance and help to people in need, but only because there is no one-for-one trade-off. If defense spending is reduced, there is no automatic shifting of those resources to humanitarian causes, and if defense spending is increased, there is no automatic reduction in spending for humanitarian concerns. The two operate in somewhat independent orbits. While in a sense they are competing for the same resources, they are also competing against a great many other competitors. For that reason, we have to discuss each of them independently rather than as part of an interrelated whole. If it were a zero-sum game and $2 billion more for defense meant $2 billion less for humanitarian purposes, then we would have to look at them together. But it is not a zero-sum game.

MR. KEMP: I agree. Les Aspin very articulately made the point that there is not a dollar-for-dollar trade-off between social or humanitarian objectives and defense spending.

Indeed, it is precisely because of our humanitarian concern for the survival of the American people and the survival of our friends and allies around the world that we are spending so much on national defense. That is humane. It seems to me that the objectives of keeping freedom alive in the world, defending the peace, and maintaining stability in the world are as humane as any other consideration one can possibly have.

The assumption of the question seems to be that we were not spending enough money in the humanitarian areas, both domestically and around the world. Of course one can always say that we are not spending enough on human goals. But I suggest that by any criterion—whether percentage of GNP, percentage of federal spending, or percentage of total federal, state, and local spending, or a comparison of spending for the last ten years on social versus defense programs—it is clear that this nation has undertaken a huge commitment to try to alleviate human misery and improve social conditions not only in America but around the world.

Finally, just take one specific measure—the budget for the Department of Health, Education, and Welfare. HEW's budget under John F. Kennedy was $15.1 billion. This current fiscal year we are looking at an HEW budget of around $160 billion. There has been a tremendous increase in social expenditures, and there has been a shift in priorities away from defense. There should not be a trade-off, because it is not an either-or situation. It is a question of what this country must do, both domestically and in defense and foreign affairs, to preserve and promote the peace and freedom of the United States and its allies.

EDWARD HUYLEBROECK, Fleet Reserve Association: I would like to shift the discussion from hardware to personnel. What impact do you think the unionization of the military would have on our defense posture and on the budget?

MR. ASPIN: As with all unionization, it would mean that wages would go up and that a job could not be eliminated for any reason. It would mean that the force structure would stay the same or get bigger and wages would go up.

Let us remember that it is the goal of all unions to protect jobs and regulate working conditions. I think unionization of the military forces would be an absolute disaster.

MR. KEMP: I strongly agree with Les, and I am very much opposed to unionization of the military. As he pointed out earlier, we are already spending a tremendous amount of our defense budget on personnel, on wages and fringe benefits, on pensions—on all the things that go into the human cost of our forces. Unionization would push these costs to astronomical heights. In addition, by doing so, it would diminish the ability of this nation to spend what is necessary in the areas that I mentioned earlier, conventional and strategic capabilities. So I join Les in total and complete opposition to such an attempt.